Fall 1982   Volume V Number 3

I0200678

Paperback Quarterly

"Journal of
Mass-Market Paperback History"

Contents

Remembering Ellery Queen
  by Angela Andrews...3

The Paperback Hall of Fame of Miscellaneous
Curiosities, Part II: Cover/Printing Variations
  by Daniel G. Roberts..10

Vardis Fisher and His Books
  by M. C. Hill...26

Reprints/Reprints: *The Hound of the Baskervilles*
  by Bill Henderson..36

The Paperback Originals of Philip K. Dick
  by Don Z. Block..44

More on P. K. Dick
  by Shawn Loudermilk...51

Letters..55

Paperback Quarterly Publications
Brownwood, Texas

Paperback Quarterly specializes in the history of mass market paperbacks.

Paperback Quarterly features articles and notes dealing with every type (mystery, detective, science fiction, western, adventure, etc) and with every aspect of new, old and rare paperbacks.

Emphasis is placed on the historical research of paperbacks, their authors, illustrators, publishers and distributors, but the editors also invite contributions of bibliographical interest. In short, the only criterion for the editors' consideration is that the subject matter pertain to paperbacks.

Paperback Quarterly pays 2ᶜ per word (200-2000 words) for articles and notes. Payment also includes two copies of the issue in which your article appears.

Paperback Quarterly is published in Spring, Summer, Fall and Winter of each year with a subscription rate of $10.00 per year or individual copies for $3.50 each. Institutional and library subscriptions are $12.00 per year. Overseas rate is $15.00. All back issues are out of print.

All correspondence, articles, notes, queries, ads and subscriptions should be sent to 1710 Vincent, Brownwood, Texas 76801. (915) 643-1182.

Ad rate card on request.

Published and Edited by

Charlotte Laughlin   Billy C. Lee

Contributing Editors

Bill Crider   Michael S. Barson
William Lyles   Thomas L. Bonn
Piet Schreuders

Printer and Technical Advisor
Martin E. Gottschalk

Copy Editor
Judy Crider

Cover logo designed by Peter Manesis

Remembering Ellery Queen
by Angela Andrews

The death last September of Frederic Dannay
(1905-1982) brought to an end the long and
successful collaboration with his cousin, Manfred
Lee (1905-1971), who had preceded him in death.

The cousins were the creators of those
popular amateur detectives, Mr. Drury Lane
"an aged Shakespearean actor with wonderful
sleuthing powers" and Mr. Ellery Queen, des-
cribed in the press releases as "the logical
successor to Sherlock Holmes." The concept of
Ellery Queen was born over lunch in 1928 when
Frederic Dannay, an advertising art director,
and Manfred Lee, a film publicist, decided to
write a mystery together and enter it in McClure's
Magazine contest. They won the contest and
even though the magazine subsequently closed
down, this first Ellery Queen mystery, "The
Roman Hat Mystery," was published in 1929 by
Frederic A. Stokes, who had co-sponsored the contest. THE FRENCH POWDER MYSTERY and THE DUTCH
SHOE MYSTERY followed in 1930 and 1931, by
which time Ellery Queen detective fiction was
enormously popular. Although it was unusual
for an author to feature in his own books, his
identity apparently remained unquestioned until
1932 when Ellery Queen was invited in person to
lecture on mystery writing at Columbia University's School of Journalism. This dilemma was
solved by a masked Frederic Dannay duly appearing as Ellery Queen. It was also in 1932 that
Viking Press published THE TRAGEDY OF X, the
first in the X Y & Z trilogy by Barnaby Ross,
another pseudonym of the Dannay and Lee writing
team. It was not long before the masked Dannay
as Ellery Queen and Lee as Barnaby Ross were
signing books in department stores and lecturing
on the merits of mystery writing. Masters of
promotion, their roles became almost inter-

THE CHINESE MYSTERY
ELLERY QUEEN

ELLERY QUEEN'S SIAMESE TWIN MYSTERY

ELLERY QUEEN
THE SPANISH CAPE MYSTERY

ELLERY QUEEN
THE DUTCH SHOE MYSTERY
The KILLER got there first!

George Mayers

Pocket Books by Ellery Queen

4

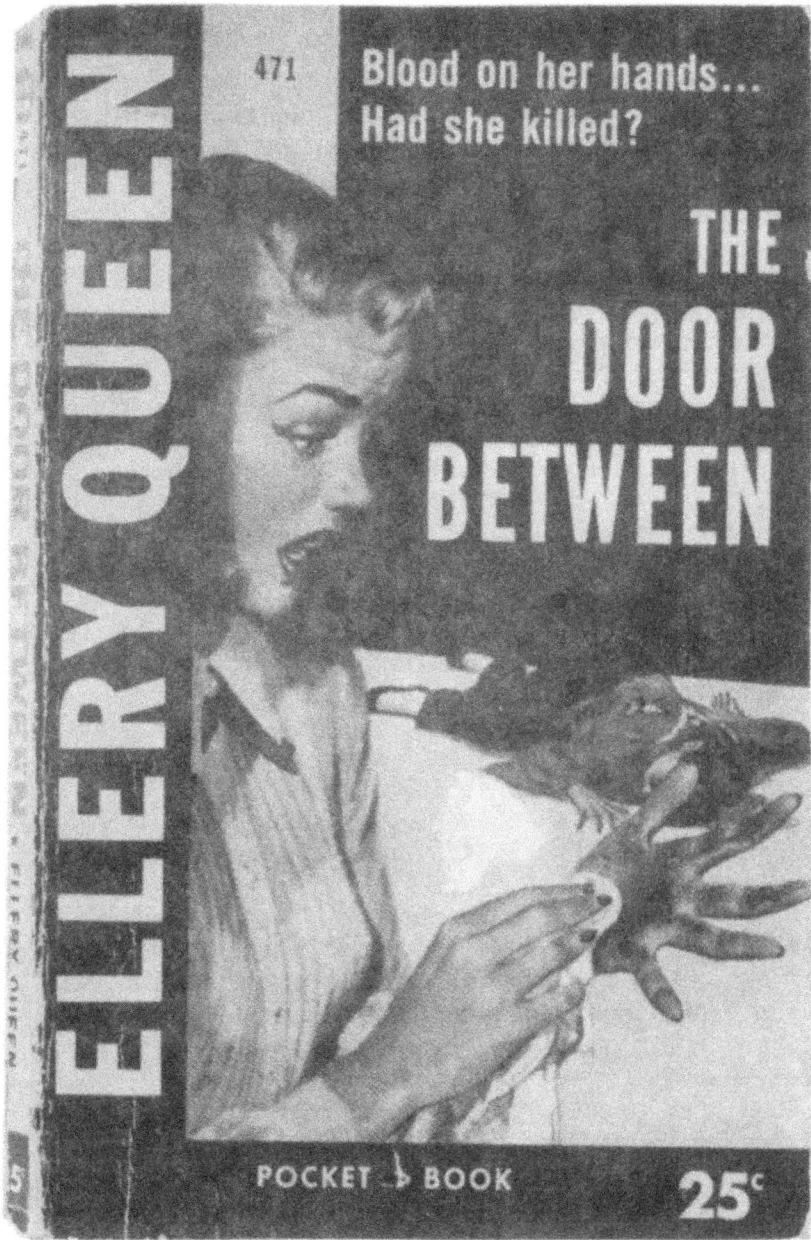

Pocket Book #471 by Ellery Queen (3rd printing)

changeable and, reputedly, they thought as one
to the point where in an Author! Author! radio
program, Dannay was Ellery and Lee was Queen.
They looked as one also in a tricky composite
photograph of them both suitably subtitled
"first photograph of Ellery Queen ever published." This photograph illustrated "the
Detective Short Story" article (by Ellery
Queen) and was timed to coincide with Little
Brown's publishing of 101 YEARS ENTERTAINMENT,
an anthology of classic detective short story
fiction drawn from the renowned Queen short
story collection.

With so much popular acclaim it was in-
evitable that Ellery Queen and Drury Lane
mysteries would find their way into paperback
books, a publishing field just beginning its
meteoric rise. Pocket Books published THE
CHINESE ORANGE MYSTERY in 1939 (Pocket Book #17),
which was an instant success. According to the
CUMULATIVE PAPERBACK INDEX, with exception of
THE AMERICAN GUN MYSTERY (Dell #4) and a Bantam
L.A. edition of THE SPANISH CAPE MYSTERY (BPLA
#1), the first 20 Ellery Queen mysteries in
paperback (including 4 by Barnaby Ross, now
ascribed to Ellery Queen) were pubished by
Pocket Books. Comet Books was later to pubish
THE GREEN TURTLE MYSTERY (Comet #13) in 1948
by Ellery Queen Jr!

Ellery Queen, as an observer, was called in
only when cases became too baffling for his
father, Inspector Queen. This armchair detective
with "the limpid eyes of the thinker" was the
life line to save the reader from floundering
too deeply. Always dependable, Queen gave
clues when necessary: in every way possible
Frederic Dannay and Manfred Lee wrote "fair
minded" mysteries surrounded by more mystery.
Their Pocket Book publishers too entered into
the spirit, and the closest explanation they
ever gave concerning the identity of "J. J.

Pocket Book #355 by Ellery Queen (1st printing)

7

McC, Northampton" who wrote all the forwards to
the Ellery Queen books was this short statement:

> In the course of the five years or so
> during which we have had the pleasure of
> publishing Mr. Queen's novels, hundreds
> of inquiries have been addressed to us
> demanding an explanation both for the
> mystery surrounding and the identity of the
> gentleman who has invariably written the
> forwords to the Queen books. We regret
> that we cannot satisfy our correspondents.
> We do not know.
>   (signed) the Publishers

It has been forty years since this statement
prefaced the foreword to THE SPANISH CAPE
MYSTERY, and since then there have been many
other books published containing both solved and
unsolved mysteries. It has been a pleasure,
Ellery Queen.

The First Twenty Ellery Queen Mysteries
Published by Pocket Books

THE CHINESE ORANGE MYSTERY (PB 17, 1939)
THE FRENCH POWDER MYSTERY (PB 71, 1940)
THE ROMAN HAT MYSTERY (PB 77, 1940)
THE ADVENTURES OF ELLERY QUEEN (PB 99, 1941)
THE SIAMESE TWIN MYSTERY (PB 109, 1941)
THE TRAGEDY OF X* (PB 125, 1941)
THE NEW ADVENTURES OF ELLERY QUEEN (PB 134, 1941)
THE SPANISH CAPE MYSTERY (PB 146, 1942)
THE GREEK COFFIN MYSTERY (PB 179, 1942)
THE DUTCH SHOE MYSTERY (PB 202, 1943)
THE EGYPTIAN CROSS MYSTERY (PB 227, 1943)
THE FOUR OF HEARTS (PB 245, 1944)
THE DEVIL TO PAY (PB 270, 1944)
CALAMITY TOWN (PB 283, 1945)
THE TRAGEDY OF Y* (PB 313, 1945)

8

THERE WAS AN OLD WOMAN (PB 326, 1946)
THE TRAGEDY OF Z* (PB 355, 1946)
DRAGON'S TEETH (PB 459, 1947)
THE DOOR BETWEEN (PB 471, 1947)
THE MURDERER IS A FOX (PB 517, 1948)

*Originally published under the pseudonym
of Barnaby Ross.

References

Queen, Ellery, CURRENT BIOGRAPHY, 1940.
"The Detective Short Story," by Ellery Queen,
    NEW YORK TIMES BOOK REVIEW, November 22, 1941.
"Ellery Queen Builds Collection of Rare Detective
    Short Stories,"PUBLISHER'S WEEKLY, November
    20, 1943.
PUBLISHER'S WEEKLY, March 24, 1951.

The Paperback Hall of Fame of Miscellaneous Curiosities, Part II: Cover/Printing Variations

by Daniel G. Roberts

This article represents the second in a three-part series on miscellaneous paperback curiosities. The first part, appearing in Paperback Quarterly Volume 5 No. 2, presented a number of examples of errata appearing in or on an assortment of paperbacks in my collection. This installment is intended to list some cover or printing variations which are known to exist. The third and final installment, to appear in Paperback Quarterly Volume 5, will outline various examples of cover art sharing.

For the purposes of this discussion, cover/ printing variations are those variations noted either in cover art or printings which are apparently inexplicable. Few of the cover variations noted below, for example, can be explained by way of different print runs, nor can any of the printing variations at this time be easily explained, at least without detailed research. It is hoped that such research may at some time be forthcoming, and that other examples of cover and/or printing variations may surface as well.

Cover/Printing Variations

1) Dell 652: Mary Roberts Rinehart, THE BAT

The front cover of this book, a Walter Brooks depiction of a winged bat framed by the moon, has at least three different color variations. In these variations, the moon and Rinehart by-line are depicted in an early day-glow rendition, either in yellow, orange, or red. Furthermore, the color variations appear to

10

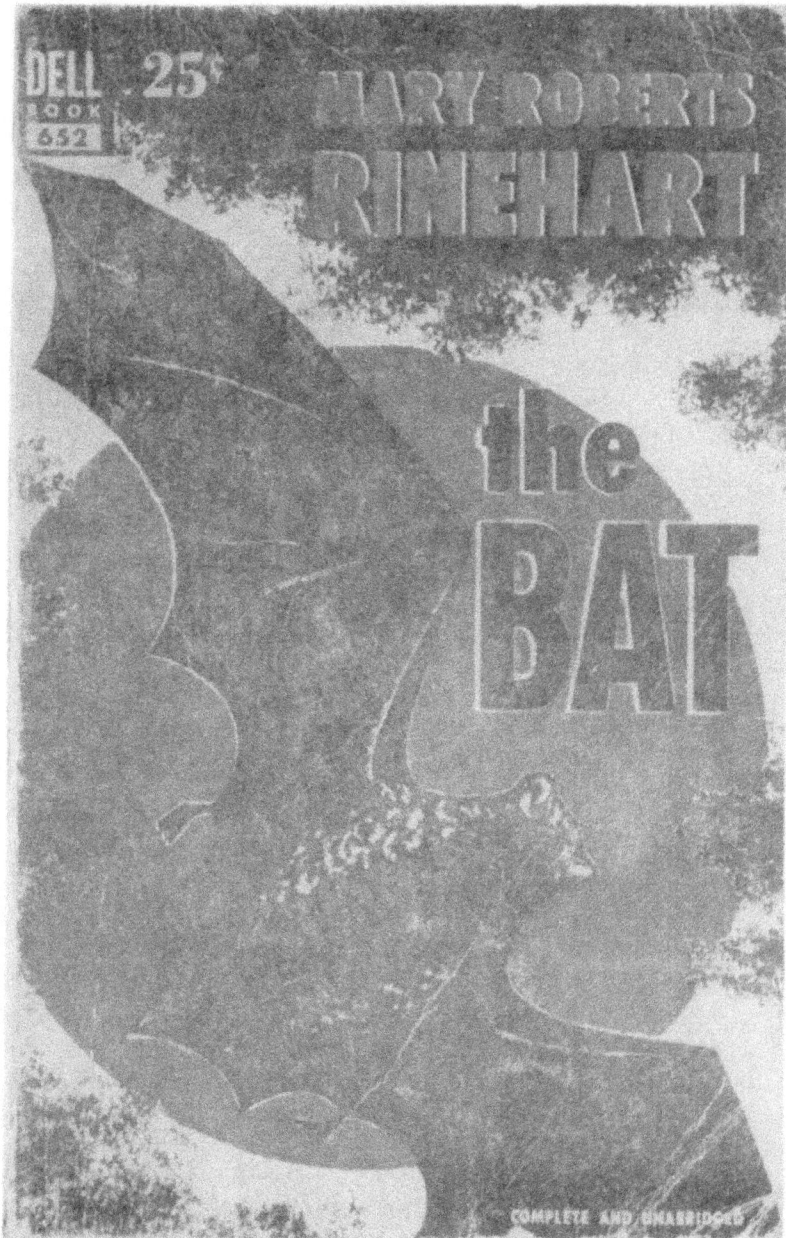

DELL 25¢
BOOK
652

MARY ROBERTS
RINEHART

the
BAT

Walter Brooks

COMPLETE AND UNABRIDGED

The Bat Dell #652--see curiosity #1

have been added to the cover at a later
stage in the manufacturing process, for a
gentle rubbing of the book's surface
suggests a color overlay. The title desig-
nation on the spine, as well as a pseudo-
circular framing of the back-cover blurb,
also appear in each of the above color
variations.

2)   Pocket Book 953: Jan de Hartog, THE SEA
     (1st printing)

     Two entirely different cover variations of
     the first printing of this Pocket book exist,
     both of which are stated to have been printed
     in August of 1953. One depicts a scuba
     diver framed in an underwater grotto, while
     the other shows a demure woman anticipating
     the advances of a gentleman with a yellow
     rose in his hand. The back covers of both
     variations are identical, as are all other
     aspects of the books.

3)   Dell 542 (1st) and 1542 (2nd): A. A. Fair,
     FOOLS DIE ON FRIDAY

     The first printing of this Donald Lam-Bertha
     Cool mystery shows a red-headed dame, with
     undergarments and breasts partially exposed,
     zipping up her skirt under the attentive
     eye of a bow-tied gent. The blurb states
     "Get your clothes on-just enough to cover
     yourself, and get out of here." Due, no
     doubt, to some adverse public reaction, the
     second printing depects the same scene,
     except that the lady is shown with the
     "offending" parts suitably covered while she
     adjusts one of her cuffs. The blurb also
     reflects the more fully-clothed state-of-
     affairs on the second printing, stating
     "You've got to get out of here! Sergeant

12

 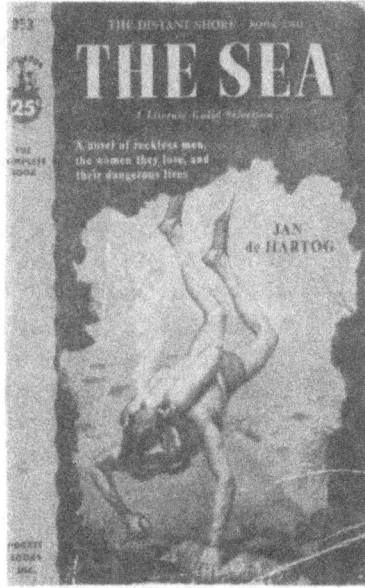

Two different cover variations of the first printing--see curiosity #2

 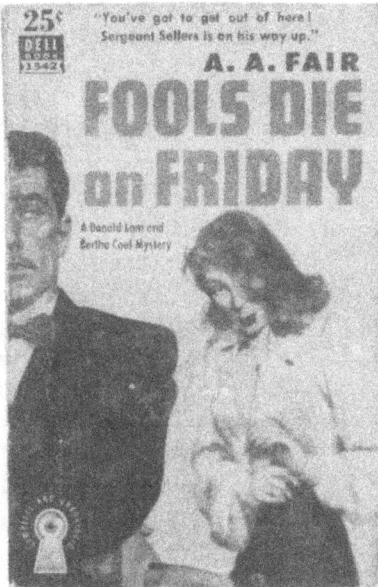

First(#542) and second(#1542) printing of *Fools Die on Friday*--
see curiosity #3

Sellers is on his way up." The artwork on
both covers is attributed to Robert Stanley.

4) Pocket Book 96: ROBERT RIPLEY, BELIEVE IT
    OR NOT! (20th printing)

    The 20th printing of this book, and possible
    other printings as well, features two subtlely
    different covers, including front cover,
    back cover, and spine. The front covers
    both show a line drawing of "The Marching
    Chinese," but graphically frame the illus-
    tration quite differently. In addition, one
    variant has a back cover blurb considerably
    abridged as compared to the other, although
    both are substantially the same blurb. The
    evolution of "Gertrude the Kanaroo" is
    also evident, since different Gertrude
    colophons appear on each variation. Finally,
    lettering style and size are considerably
    different on each version. One wonders
    how many of the earlier printings of this
    Pocket Book exhibit similar variations.

5) Collier AS147: Anthony Boucher, THE CASE
    OF THE BAKER STREET IRREGULARS

    This excellent Sherlockian pastiche features
    at least two different color variations on
    both the front and back covers. Both
    feature line drawings of a deerstalker, pipe,
    and magnifying glass, with a bright red
    background. In one version, however, the
    deerstalker is rendered in green ink while
    in the other, it is rendered in orange.
    The same color variation is evident as well
    on a small rectangle upon which the front-
    cover blurb appears.

6) Dell First Edition B142: POKER ACCORDING
    TO MAVERICK

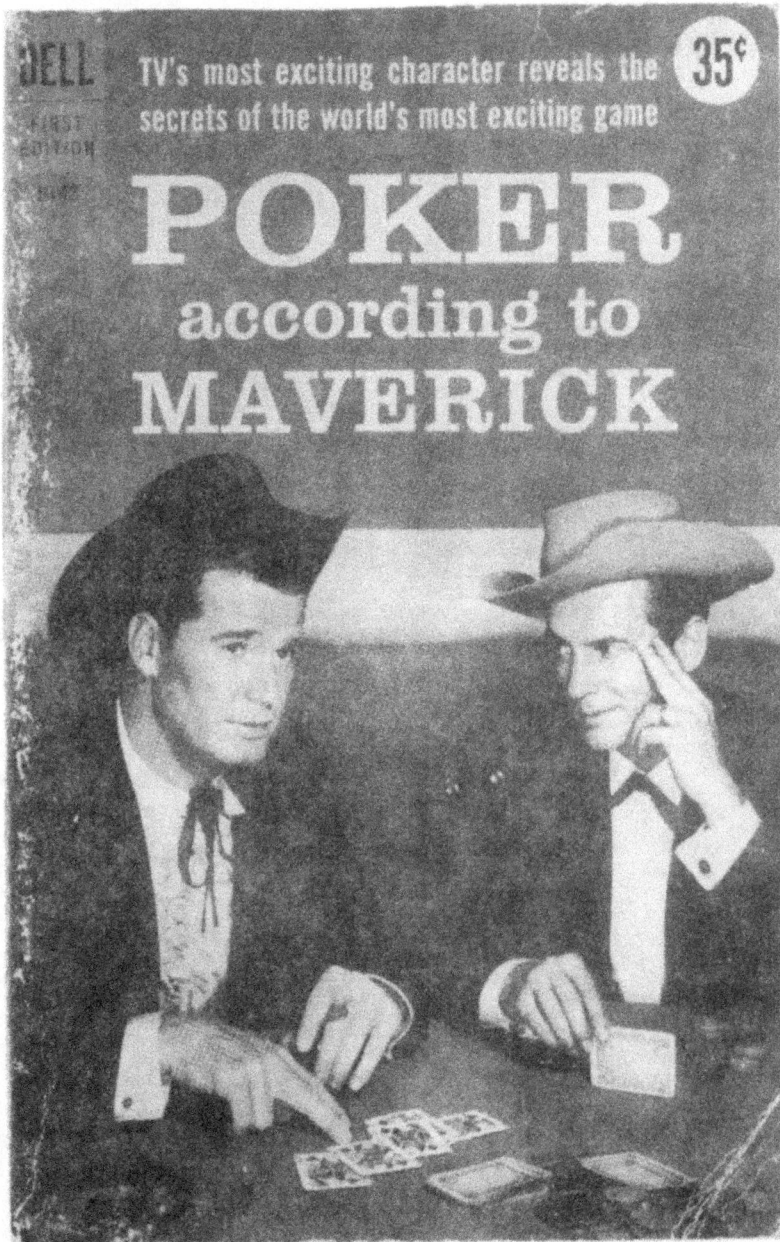

Front cover of *Poker According to Maverick*--see curiosity #6

Four different back covers for *Poker According to Maverick*-- see curiosity #6

There are at least four different back covers
associated with the first and second printings.
The first edition of this book, appearing in
October 1959, featured advertisements on the
back cover, but at least two different ads
are noted, including one pushing four clean-
ing products of the Drackett Company and
"Maverick," under the byline "Five of a Kind,"
while the other entices the reading public
to buy a Jeep. The second printing, appearing in March 1960, features neither of the
advertisements noted above. Instead, two
different versions exist, including one which
plugs Kaiser Aluminum & Chemical Sales, Inc.
on an otherwise blank background, and another
extolling the virtues of learning to play
poker in the "Maverick tradition" by reading
the book. In all other aspects, the books
appear to be identical. Are there any other
variations to the Maverick back cover?

7) Pocket Book 212: Raymond Chandler, FAREWELL
MY LOVELY (10th printing)

Once again, two radically different cover
variations are noted for a Pocket Book, in
this case the 10th printing of Chandler's
classic detective novel. The one variation
depicts an excellent H. L. Hoffman cover
painting of a dapper gent illuminated by
night-time neon, a cover which, to the best
of my knowledge, appeared on the first nine
printings as well. The other sports a
rather violent Paul Kresse cover, taken from
a scene in the novel, in which a bedspring
is being "smashed ... against his cheek."
Interestingly and inexplicably, the latter
indicates a 10th printing date of April 1951,
while the former indicates the 10th printing
took place in September 1945. Similarly, not
all of the earlier print-run information

17

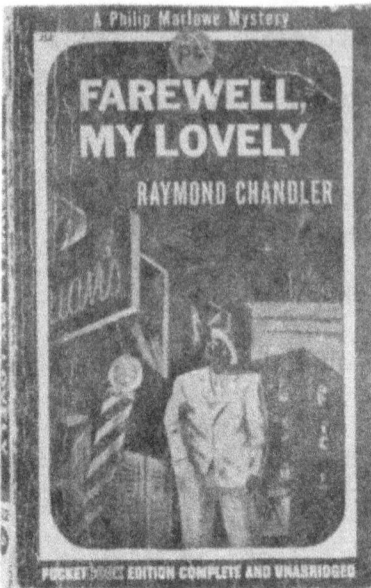
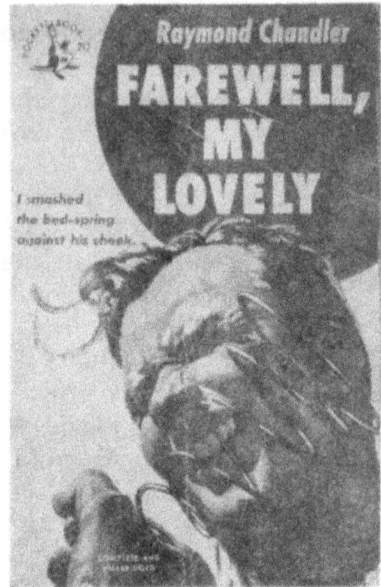

Two different covers for the 10th printing of *Farewell My Lovely*--see curiosity #7

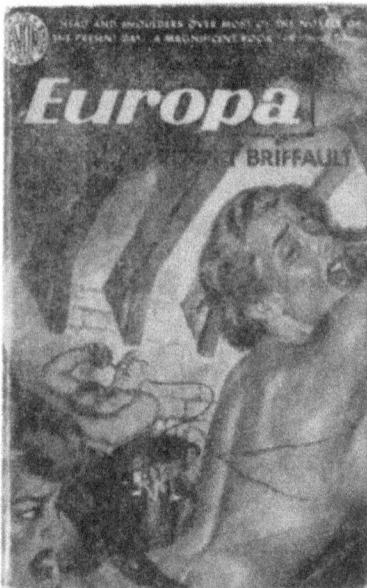

Avon #272 -- Two different covers exist for this Robert Briffault book--see curiosity #10

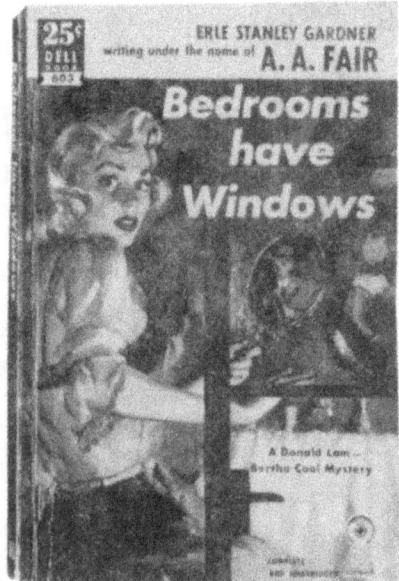

Dell #603--Two different covers exist for this A.A. Fair book--see curiosity #12

coincides. There appears to have been some confusion at Pocket Books with the printing history of this volume.

8) Pocket Book 524 and 2524: Roy Huggins, THE DOUBLE TAKE

The original William Morrow hardback edition of this hardboiled novel (from which 77 Sunset Strip was launched), was printed in 1945, also coinciding with the time that the action in the novel takes place. Pocket Book 524, the first Pocket edition, printed in June 1948, remains faithful to the original time period. The second printing (number 2524, July 1959), however, has all dates changed in the text to reflect a "present" of 1959. The copyright page of number 2524 also states "This Pocket Book includes every word contained in the original, higher-priced edition..." Well, indeed that is true, if the numerous references to dates and years are not considered to be words!

9) Pocket Book 23: THE AUTOBIOGRAPHY OF BENJAMIN FRANKLIN (1st and 5th printings)

While there are no noticeable cover variations on the 1st and 5th printings of this autobiography, the contents vary remarkably. The 1st appears to be a watered-down version of the 5th and, in fact, has some 100 pages less in its contents. Without subjecting both editions to detailed readings (one of those I choose not to read), the only clue to this major discrepancy appears on the title page, of the 5th printing, which indicates that there also are included therein "Sayings of Poor Richard, Hoaxes, Bagatelles, Essays, and Letters, selected and edited by

19

Carl Van Doren," while the title page of the 1st says no such thing and, accordingly, does not include them. In point of fact, however, this is not the only difference, since a perusal of the first few pages of the auto-biographical part, allegedly in Franklin's own words, reveals that the 1st and 5th printings contain considerably different transcriptions of Franklin's text. Since the front covers indicate that both the 1st and 5th printings are "Complete and Un-abridged," I would be most interested to see an incomplete and/or abridged version. It would also be interesting to compare other printings of the same book, in particular the 2nd, 3rd, and 4th printings.

10)   Avon 272:   Robert Briffault, EUROPA

As most Avon collectors are aware, two entirely different front cover illustrations exist for the Avon edition of this 1930's novel of European decadence. One cover illustration shows the bust (from the neck up only) of an aristocratic young lady framed by a background map of Europe. The other cover consists of a classic "bondage" cover, in which a macho bald-headed thug whips a naked and bound damsel. Needless to say, the latter variation is more widely sought by collectors than the former. While the lettering and design of the spines of both books are also slightly different, the books are identical in all other aspects.

11)   Avon 169 and 300:   Irving Shulman, THE AMBOY DUKES

At least three different cover variations exist for the first and second Avon printings of this classic juvenile delinquency novel. The first printing of number 169 shows a

In the many years since the "Shakespeare-Head" first appeared as the imprint on Avon Books, millions of readers have found that this trademark represents a high standard of reading entertainment. Because every Avon title is selected primarily for maximum reading pleasure, Avon Books have attained a wide popularity among the great American reading public.

In these days of continual rising prices in almost every sphere of purchasing, Avon Pocket-Size Books remain at their pre-war price of 25c. This is an amazing book-buying value that you can't afford to overlook.

Look for the SHAKESPEARE HEAD imprint on the title page

Two different cover variations for Avon #169--see curiosity #11

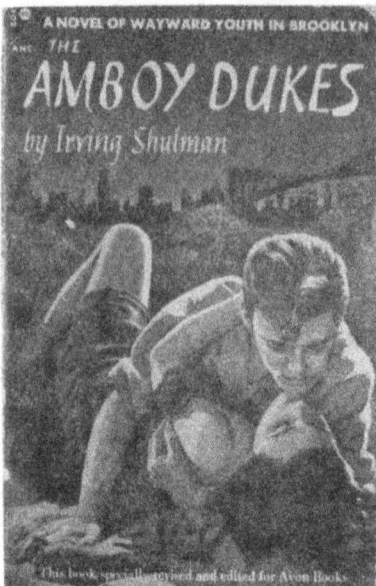

"This Book Is Emphatically a Reading 'Must' for Young People . . ."

EDWIN J. LUKAS, EXECUTIVE DIRECTOR
SOCIETY FOR THE PREVENTION OF CRIME (NEW YORK)

This book is emphatically a reading "must" for young people as well as for the sociologist interested in the phenomena of gang warfare and neighborhood tensions. The saga of a conflict gang, told so powerfully in THE AMBOY DUKES, is really twice told: once, within the covers of this book; and again, in every city and town of the U.S.A. Rarely has a writer captured so faithfully and recorded so excitingly the poignant drama that is being daily unfolded for hundreds of thousands of our young people in the teeming pathways we call "streets."

Within the compass of every city street are found eloquent evidence of all of society's strengths and weaknesses—from the towering air-conditioned edifices of industry to the filthy dwelling places provided for man to lay his weary body at day's end; from youth's craving for understanding, sympathy and affection, to the community's indifference to those needs. The street bears the tokens of all our ambitions, hopes, and capacity to love and be loved. But there are also the scars of our fears, hates, envy, thirst for revenge, and the deep, tortured feelings of guilt which arise out of long forgotten as well as remembered episodes.

When and how can we bring these forces under control? It will, or should be, clear to the readers of THE AMBOY DUKES that they have it within their power to strike a telling blow against the continuance of the conditions—economic, social and psychological—which breed and foster crime.

Edwin J. Lukas,
Executive Director
Society for the Prevention of Crime

"THIS BOOK IS EMPHATICALLY A READING 'MUST' FOR YOUNG PEOPLE..."

Edwin J. Lukas, Executive Director,
SOCIETY FOR THE PREVENTION OF CRIME (NEW YORK)

This book is emphatically a reading "must" for young people as well as for the sociologist interested in the phenomena of gang warfare and neighborhood tensions. The saga of a conflict gang, told so powerfully in THE AMBOY DUKES, is really twice told: once, within the covers of this book; and again, in every city and town of the U.S.A. Rarely has a writer captured so faithfully and recorded so excitingly the poignant drama that is being daily unfolded for hundreds of thousands of our young people in the teeming pathways we call "streets."

Within the compass of every city street are found eloquent evidences of all of society's strengths and weaknesses—from the towering air-conditioned edifices of industry to the filthy dwelling places provided for man to lay his weary body at day's end; from youth's craving for understanding, sympathy and affection, to the community's indifference to those needs. The street bears the tokens of all our ambitions, hopes, and capacity to love and be loved. But there are also the scars of our fears, hates, envy, thirst for revenge, and the deep, tortured feelings of guilt which arise out of long forgotten as well as remembered episodes.

When and how can we bring these forces under control? It will, or should be, clear to the readers of THE AMBOY DUKES that they have it within their power to strike a telling blow against the continuance of the conditions—economic, social and psychological—which breed and foster crime.

Edwin J. Lukas, Executive Director,
Society for the Prevention of Crime

Two different cover variations for Avon #300--see curiosity #11

young tough and his lady friend in a passionate embrace with the Manhattan skyline as a
backdrop. The back cover features a standard Avon blurb extolling the merits of Avon
books in general, and makes no mention of
Shulman's title. The second printing of
number 169 capitalizes on the release of the
Universal Pictures film, showing a still
from the film on the back cover. The front
cover, as well, is totally different,
featuring a young hood, cigarette dangling
from mouth, and his girlfriend leaning
against a wall. A blurb advertising the
film also occurs on the front cover.
Similarly, Avon number 300 also exhibits
the same front cover variations, with one
showing the same hood and girl leaning
against the same wall, and the other showing the passionate embrace framed by the
Manhattan skyline. However, neither
version of No. 300 shows the standard Avon
back cover blurb occurring on the first
printing of number 169 nor the movie still
occurring on the back of the second printing
of number 169. Instead, in different for-
mats, a lengthy statement by Edwin J. Lukas,
Executive Director of the Society for the
Prevention of Crime appears, in which the
praises of "The Amboy Dukes" are duly sung.
Are there any other variations of this
Avon title?

12) Dell 603: A. A. Fair, BEDROOMS HAVE WINDOWS

This Dell title has at least two front cover
variations, even though the central illustration, a Mike Ludlow work depicting a
startled woman with a hand-held mirror in
which an intruder is framed, is identical.
On one version, a one-inch yellow band, in
which the A. A. Fair byline appears,

frames the illustration at the top, while
on the other, the artwork extends all the
way to the top margin. In addition, the
yellow-banded version frames all elements
of the logo (i.e., "25¢," "Dell Book,"
and "603") in a single rectangle, while on
the other variation, the "25¢" appears
outside of the box, at the top. Although
no printing information is provided, one
suspects one version postdates the other.

13) Novel Library 7: Jack Woodford, GROUNDS
FOR DIVORCE

Two different color variations of the front
cover illustration, which depicts a passionate heterosexual embrace in vintage Novel
Library style, are known for this title.
In both, the background depicts what appears
to be either an expansive lake or desert,
but one version is rendered in blue-green
while the other is rendered in a sandy
yellow or light tan color. Since the
pictorial details are vague, perhaps the
color variations are intended to connote
water, in the one case, and desert sand
in the other.

14) Pocket Book 596: Bennett Cerf (ed.), TRY
AND STOP ME

The first printing (February 1949) of this
collection fo humor has at least two
distinctly different front cover variations.
One duplicates the Leo Manso design appearing on the dustjacket of the Simon and
Schuster first edition, in which the title
"Try and Stop Me" appears with four small
humorous line drawings. The other depicts
a black and white photograph of the hard
cover edition, but under the title "Bennett
Cerf's Collection of Humorous Anecdotes and

Short Stories." The latter also indicates
"New Revised Edition," instead of the "Newly
Revised Edition" of the former. Except for
slight variations in the spine design, as
well as the fact that the latter indicates
on the back cover that the front cover
disign is by Leo Manso, the books are
otherwise apparently identical.

Acknowledgments

I wish to thank Bob Gray, Ina Cooke, and
Paul Herman, each of whom pointed out at least
one variation presented herein. In addition, it
should be noted that the Dell 542 and 1542 cover
variations previously have been presented by Bill
Lyles in Collecting Paperbacks? 1(2):12, by
Piet Schreuders in his book, PAPERBACKS, U.S.A.:
A GRAPHIC HISTORY, 1939-1959, pp. 109-110, and
by Thomas Bonn in his book UNDERCOVER, p. 56.
The Avon 272 and 169/300 variations, as well as
the Dell B142 variations, were noted by Kevin
Hancer in his PAPERBACK PRICE GUIDE No. 2 on
pp. 52, 49 and 53, and 181, respectively. Two
of the Dell B142 variations were also noted by
Barry Pattengill in Collecting Paperbacks?
2(4):1, and Wally Pattengill provided assistance
in further clarifying the latter.

---Daniel Roberts
518 Marshall Dr.
West Chester, Penn.   19380

Vardis Fisher and His Books
by M. C. Hill

A unique series of stories long out of
print was produced by Vardis Fisher, a son of
the pioneering wilderness. Born in Annis,
Idaho, on March 31, 1895, to newly converted
Mormons, he grew up in what was still frontier
America, witnessing wildlife, Indians, bad men
and the early growth of the West in all its
aspects. He was able to store up thousands of
facts, experiences and memories that would
later be incorporated into many of his novels
dealing with primitive life on the American
frontier.

Fisher's parents were instrumental in
disciplining him to a life of learning and gave
him a desire to obtain a good education,
which bore fruit in his receiving a Bachelor
of Arts degree from the University of Idaho.

While attending the university he was
exposed to other young men proficient in the
art of writing who convinced him that he had
the ability to write. But having a more urgent
desire to go on further with his education,
he entered the University of Chicago where he
received both Master of Arts and Doctor of
Philosophy degrees.

He then applied for and received approval
to teach at the University of Utah and later
at New York University. For the next 11 years
he settled into a regular routine which gave
him time to start honing his writing talents,
researching, studying and preparing to write
the great novel. During the lean years of the
depression, he also did some newspaper work
for a Salt Lake City daily and when able to,
he also wrote some technical papers for the
federal government.

In 1927, he wrote his first book for

Pyramid Royal #R419 by Vardis Fisher

publication (SONNETT TO AN IMAGINARY MADONNA)
which was produced in such small quantities
that it is almost impossible to locate a
copy today.
    The following is a complete chronological
list of everything Fisher wrote. The titles
with an asterisk appeared in paperback.

1927   SONNETT TO AN IMAGINARY MADONNA
1928   TOILERS OF THE HILLS
1931 *DIRK BRIDWELL. Reprinted in paperback as
      THE WILD ONES. Pyramid G57(1952),
      Pyramid G141 (1955), Pyramid G310 (1958).
1932 *IN TRAGIC LIFE. Reprinted in paperback
      by Cardinal (C-3) in 1951.
1934 *PASSIONS SPIN THE PLOT. Reprinted in paper-
      by Cardinal (C-73) in 1952.
1935 *WE ARE BETRAYED. Reprinted in paperback
      by Cardinal (C-119) in 1953.
1935   THE NEUOTIC NIGHTINGALE
1936 *NO VILLAIN NEED BE. Reprinted in paperback
      by Cardinal (C-177) in 1955.
1937   APRIL
1937   FORGIVE US OUR VIRTUES
1937   ODYSSEY OF A HERO
1939   CHILDREN OF GOD (THE MORMON TREK)--won the
      1939 Harper novel prize.
1941 *THE MOTHERS. Reprinted in paperback as
      THE DONNER PARTY STORY by Pyramid T1242.
1943 *DARKNESS AND THE DEEP. Reprinted in
      paperback by Pyramid (R527) in 1960.
1944 *THE GOLDEN ROOMS. Reprinted in paperback
      by Pyramid (R472) in 1960.
1946 *INTIMATIONS OF EVE. Reprinted in paperback
      by Pyramid (R657) in 1961.
1947 *ADAM AND THE SERPENT. Reprinted in paper-
      back by Pyramid (R677) in 1961.
1948 *THE DIVINE PASSION. Reprinted in paper-
      back by Pyramid (R419) in 1959.
1951 *VALLEY OF VISION. Reprinted in paperback
      by Pyramid (R597) in 1961.

An elemental story of untamed emotions

THE
WILD
ONES

(Original Title: Dark Bridwell)

Vardis Fisher

"Powerful!"—New York Times

Gerald Powell

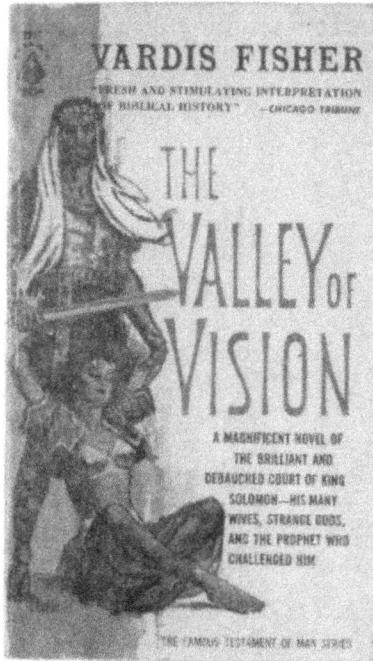

VARDIS FISHER

"FRESH AND STIMULATING INTERPRETATION
OF BIBLICAL HISTORY" —CHICAGO TRIBUNE

THE
VALLEY OF
VISION

A MAGNIFICENT NOVEL OF
THE BRILLIANT AND
DEBAUCHED COURT OF KING
SOLOMON—HIS MANY
WIVES, STRANGE GODS,
AND THE PROPHET WHO
CHALLENGED HIM

THE FAMOUS TESTAMENT OF MAN SERIES

Victor Kalin

ADAM AND
THE SERPENT

The famous
TESTAMENT OF MAN
series

Jack Thurston

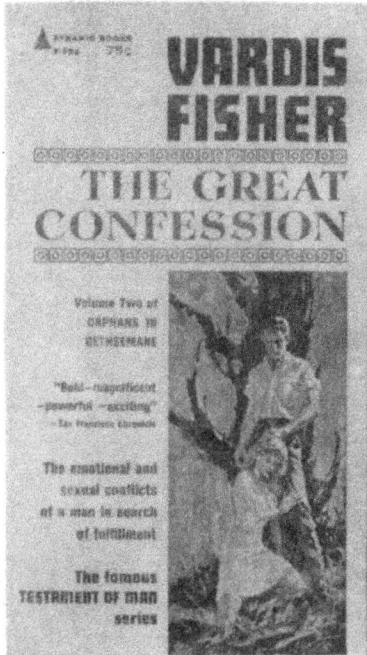

**VARDIS
FISHER**

THE GREAT
CONFESSION

Volume Two of
ORPHANS IN
GETHSEMANE

"Bold—magnificent
—powerful —exciting"
—San Francisco Chronicle

The emotional and
sexual conflicts
of a man in search
of fulfillment

The famous
TESTAMENT OF MAN
series

Jack Thurston

Pyramid books by Vardis Fisher

1952 *ISLAND OF THE INNOCENT. Reprinted in
        paperback by Pyramid (R629) in 1961.
1953 GOD OR CAESAR.
1956 *PEMMICAN. Reprinted in paperback as
        THE HUDSON BAY CO. STORY by Cardinal
        (C-253).
1956 *JESUS CAME AGAIN. Reprinted in paperback
        by Pyramid (X716) in 1962.
1956 *A GOAT FOR AZAZEL. Reprinted in paperback
        by Pyramid (X705) in 1962.
1957 *THE PASSION WITHIN. Reprinted in paperback
        by Pyramid (R522) as PEACE LIKE A RIVER.
1958 TALE OF VALOR.
1960 LOVE AND DEATH (Complete short stories)
1962 THOMAS WOLFE AS I KNEW HIM
1962 *FOR PASSION, FOR HEAVEN.   Printed in
        paperback by Pyramid (T746) in 1962.
1962 *THE GREAT CONFESSION.   Printed in paper-
        back by Pyramid (T756) in 1962.
1963 SUICIDE OR MURDER (The strange death of
        Governor Meriwether Lewis).
1965 *MOUNTAIN MEN. Pocket Book #75211.
1968 GOLD RUSHES AND MINING CAMPS OF THE EARLY
        AMERICAN WEST.

        In 1943, publisher Alan Swallow issued
DARKNESS AND THE DEEP, the first of one of the
most unpublicized series of books ever to be
offered to the book-buying public. Vardis
Fisher started to write this book back in the
early thirties but found that it was going to
be too much for one volume. He spent at least
six years researching through libraries before
he settled on the fact that if he were ever
going to complete this saga he would have to
spread it out over a number of years and volumes.
As it turned out he was lucky to get it all in
the thirteen volumes. Before he was through
with the last volume, he had spent seventeen
long years, finishing the series in 1960.
        The following is a complete list of the

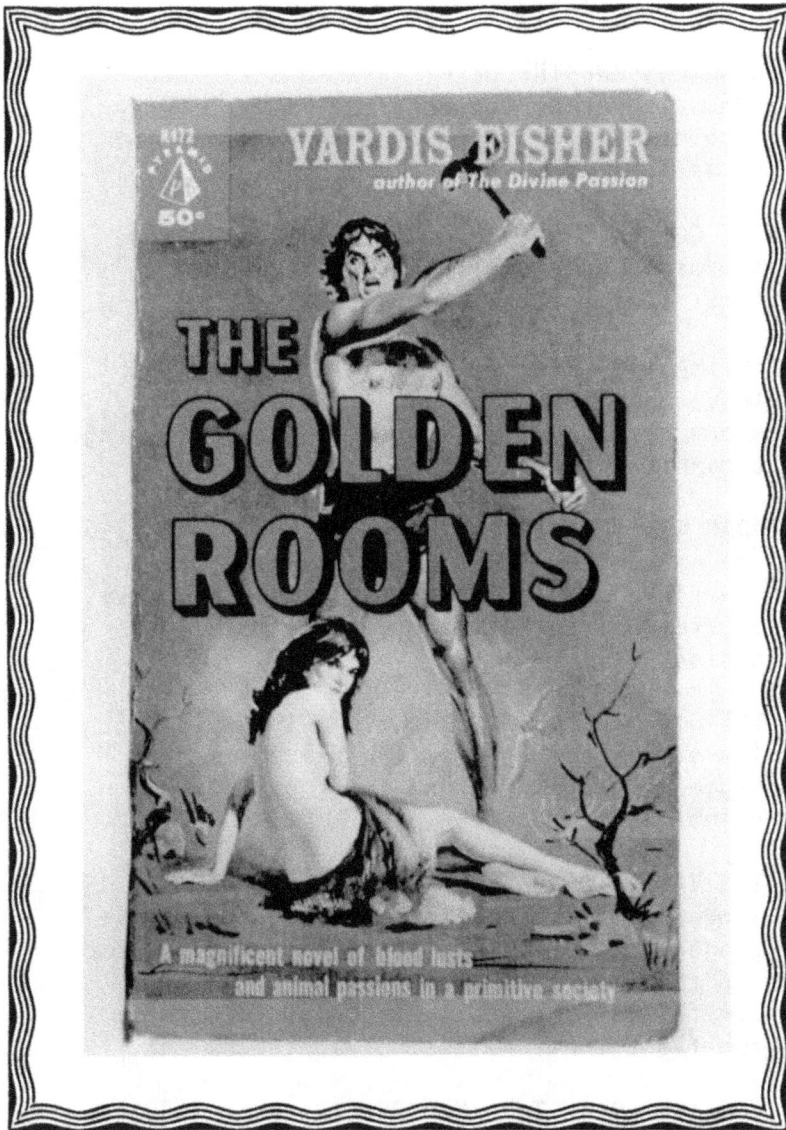

The Golden Rooms by Vardis Fisher (Pyramid R472)

series with publisher, number, date and cover artist.

"The Testament of Man Series"

1 DARKNESS AND THE DEEP, Pyramid R527, Aug. 1960. (cover by Bob Schultz) This gives an account of pre-historic man's discovery of himself.

2 THE GOLDEN ROOMS, Pyramid R472, Jan. 1960. (cover by Bob Maguire) This recounts man's first sense of the supernatural.

3 INTIMATIONS OF EVE, Pyramid R657, Oct. 1961. (cover by Jack Thurston) This tells the story of Raven and his facing the dominating, tyrannical female.

4 ADAM AND THE SERPENT, Pyramid R677, Dec. 1961. (cover by Jack Thurston) This tells the powerful, passionate story of the primative, matriarchal society and of man's revolt against it.

5 THE DIVINE PASSION, Pyramid R419, July 1959 (cover by Bob Maguire) This exposes the pagan men and women and their primative, uninhibited sex-worship.

6 THE VALLEY OF VISION, Pyramid R597, March 1961. (cover by Victor Kalin) Relates the battle of giants, the powerful, passionate King Solomon and the dedicated, fiery, prophet Elijah. Strife, famine, and death occur when these two fight their battle for supremacy.

7 THE ISLAND OF THE INNOCENT, Pyramid R629, July 1961. (cover by Gino Forte) This is the story of Philemon the handsome Greek doctor that meets Judith the pious daughter of Israel.

8   JESUS CAME AGAIN, Pyramid X176, April 1962.
     (cover by Jack Thurston) This is the story
     of Joshua the Jew --a novel of sin and
     salvation in a licentious world.

9   A GOAT FOR AZAZEL, Pyramid X705, March 1962.
     (cover by Gino Forte) This is the fascin-
     ating odyssey of a young Roman (Dawson) who
     sated himself in the dissolute world of the
     first century, until he finally finds the
     goal of his quest for love in a new and
     sublime experience.

10   THE PASSION WITHIN (PEACE LIKE A RIVER),
     Pyramid R522, July 1960. (cover by Bob
     Maguire) This tells of Horeb who sought out
     the most beautiful of all harlots, Thais,
     the one no man had ever been able to resist.

11   MY HOLY SATAN, Pyramid R546, Oct. 1960.
     (cover by Victor Kalin) This is a brilliant
     portrayal of one of the basest ages of
     civilized man--the story of Richard's fight
     for love and freedom in the feudal age.

12   FOR PASSION, FOR HEAVEN, Pyramid T746, July
     1962. (cover by Jack Thurston) Book 1 Orphans
     of Gethsemane. This brings Vridar Hunter
     into the 1920s and tells of his tormented
     struggle with sin, sex and society. (Note:
     Fisher wrote a trilogy featuring Vridar Hunter
     in the 1930s starting with IN A TRAGIC LIFE,
     then PASSIONS SPIN THE PLOT and WE ARE BE-
     TRAYED. I would suggest that if you are
     going to read any of this series, that you
     read them in their proper order so that you
     can follow the author's growth as he completes
     each new offering.)

13   THE GREAT CONFESSIONS, Pyramid T756, Aug. 1962.
     (cover by Jack Thurston) This brings us to the
     end of the series with Vridar Hunter still

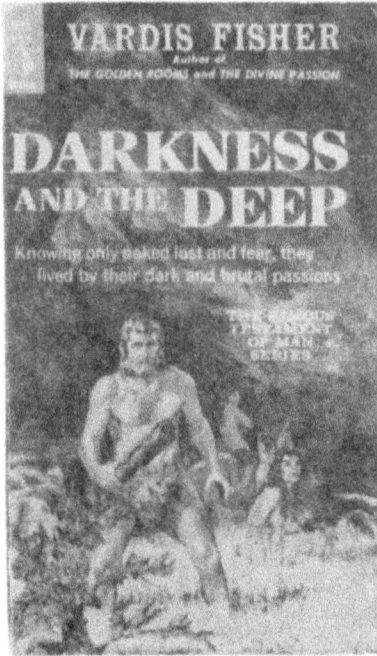

VARDIS FISHER
Author of
THE GOLDEN ROOMS and THE DIVINE PASSION

DARKNESS
AND THE DEEP

Knowing only naked lust and fear, they
lived by their dark and brutal passions

THE FAMOUS
TESTAMENT
OF MAN
SERIES

Bob Schulz

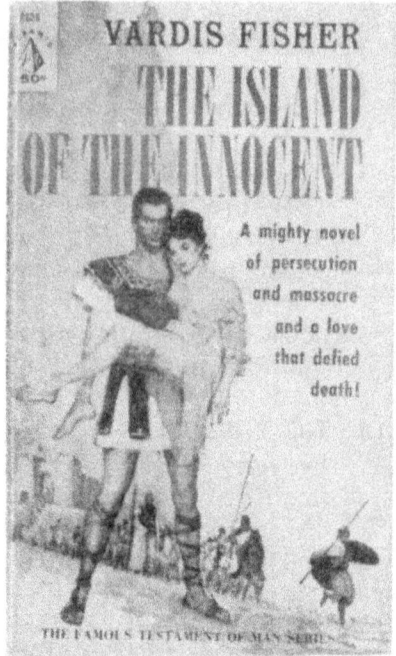

VARDIS FISHER

THE ISLAND
OF THE INNOCENT

A mighty novel
of persecution
and massacre
and a love
that defied
death!

THE FAMOUS TESTAMENT OF MAN SERIES

Gino Forte

VARDIS FISHER

Sin and self-torture—a powerful
novel of lust and renunciation
at the dawn of the Christian era.

The PASSION
WITHIN

Original title: Peace Like a River

THE FAMOUS
TESTAMENT
OF MAN
SERIES

Bob Maguire

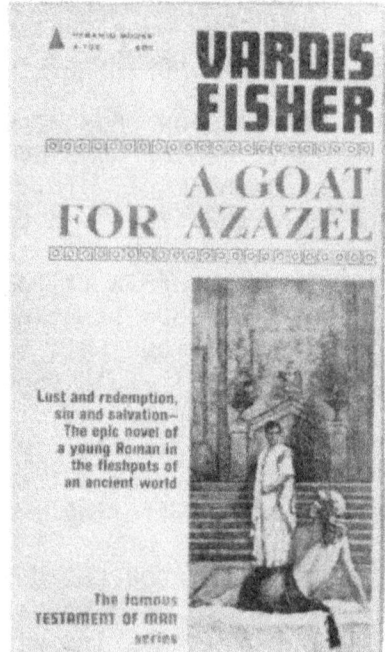

VARDIS
FISHER

A GOAT
FOR AZAZEL

Lust and redemption,
sin and salvation—
The epic novel of
a young Roman in
the fleshpots of
an ancient world

The famous
TESTAMENT OF MAN
series

Gino Forte

Pyramid books by Vardis Fisher

34

searching for the truth and for the woman
that will fulfill his urgent, human needs.
It is the unforgetable story of love, life
and thought.

Most of the paperback titles went into two to
five different printings, so when you uncover any
of the series titles they will generally turn out
to be second printings or later. Different
printings had different covers painted by a
variety of people. I find that Jack Thurston
painted most of the second, third and fourth
printings covers.

Only one title was printed by the
Armed Services Editions. THE GOLDEN ROOMS was
printed as #713 on September 1945--125,000 copies
were produced. Try and locate one today.

Reprints/Reprints:
The Hound of the Baskervilles
by Bill Henderson

Sherlock Holmes, without a doubt, has become one of the legendary characters in literature. And though over ninety years old, Doyle's world-renowned character never becomes outdated and is periodically introduced to a new generation of fans by various paperback publishers.

Sherlock Holmes's "most famous case," as the blurb on the first mass market Doyle paperback declares, is THE HOUND OF THE BASKERVILLES (Bantam #366). This first Sherlock Holmes paperback was published in 1949. The cover illustrator for the first mass market paperback edition was William Shoyer who worked for Bantam between 1948 and 1950. The cover for this edition was Shoyer's first cover for Bantam. And this was Bantam's only "Hound" publishing venture.

It was ten years later in August 1959 before THE HOUND OF THE BASKERVILLES was released again, this time by Dell in their Great Mystery Library series as Dell D302-35¢. The cover features a deerstalker, pipe, magnifying glass and a threatening letter featured in the story. William Teason, who did all the covers for the Dell Great Mystery Library series, drew the cover illustration.

Dell ran THE HOUND OF THE BASKERVILLES through at least 12 printings and along the way transferred it to Dell's Laurel-leaf Library edition--Dell 3758, 45¢, 12th printing. This 1969 edition features a close-up of a red-eyed, hound's head surrounded by a dense fog. An affective cover by an artist unknown to me.

Though Dell's printing history of THE HOUND OF THE BASKERVILLES spans ten years, other paperback publishers were also active. In 1963, Berkley released "the Hound" in what they publicized on their front cover as the "author-

Teason

Dell D302-35¢

Dell 3758-45¢

Berkley s2695-75¢

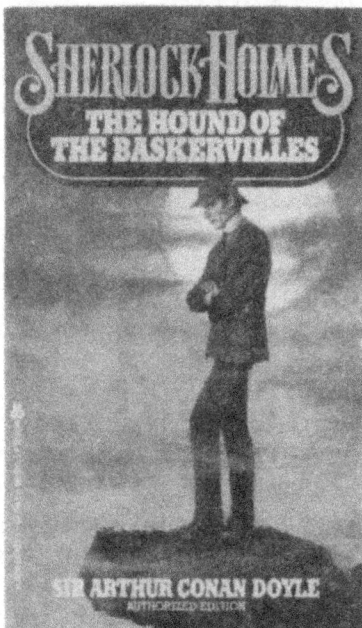

Berkley 04421-$1.95

ized edition." On their copyright page, they state "published by agreement with The Sir Arthur Conan Doyle Estates." Berkley is the only paperback publisher I have found that denotes such permission except the 12th printing of the Dell Laurel Leaf Library edition. Since this 1963 edition, Berkley has kept THE HOUND OF THE BASKERVILLES in print. Their first printing (Berkely Medallion F858) sold for 50¢ and by their 8th printing in 1971 the price had been raised to 75¢ but still had the same cover. The cover features a leafless tree above a thick fog with a deerstalker, magnifying glass, pipe, gun, and skull beneath or in the tree. By Berkley's 23rd printing (September 1980), the cover featured a tall, arms-folded-in-thought Sherlock Holmes standing on a boulder, overlooking a cliff. A large moon is behind the detective and a dense fog is all around him.

While Dell was printing THE HOUND OF THE BASKERVILLES between 1959 and 1969 and Berkley between 1963 and 1980, still other paperback publishers were finding markets for their own editions. In March 1964, Scholastic Book Services released their first printing with an excellent Mort Kunstler cover. This first printing (T590-45¢) features the ruins of an old building with dead trees all around. Through a window of the ruined building the reader can see a howling hound on the misty horizon. Scholastic Book Services 8th printing (December 1969), however, features the poorest "Hound" cover I have seen yet: a man in the foreground wearing pre-Victorian clothes (which is certainly out of place in this novel) with a hound in the background baying at the huge moon above. The cover has a muted blue appearance, probably an attempt to imitate a dense fog--it just doesn't work. The book number for this 8th printing is also T590 but sold for 60¢. And though the printing plates for this edition are the same as

Mort Kunstler

Scholastic T590-45¢

Mort Kunstler?

Scholastic T590-60 ¢

A Dale Classic

Lancer Magnum Easy Eye

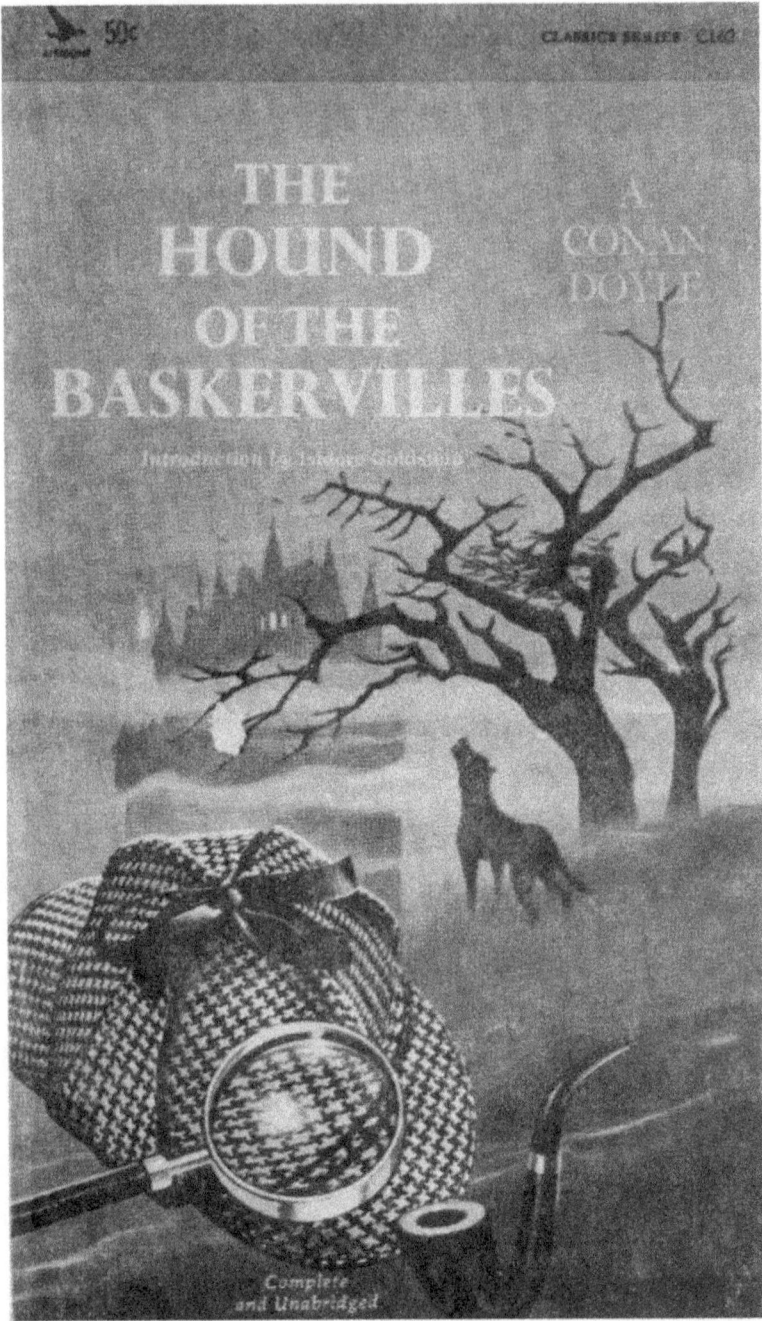

THE
HOUND
OF THE
BASKERVILLES

A
CONAN
DOYLE

Introduction by Isidore Goldstein

Complete
and Unabridged

Airmont Classic Series CL62

Scholastic's first printing which gives Mort
Kunstler the cover credit, I don't believe
Kunstler did this 8th printing.

The next paperback publisher to publish
THE HOUND OF THE BASKERVILLES was Airmont Publishing in their Classic Series (CL62-50¢) This
is the first edition since the Bantam #366 edition
to declare on the front cover, "Complete and
Unabridged." One can quickly understand why
Airmont decided to convey this message to the
reader since the volume is so thin (128 pages)
that the next closest edition has almost 50
pages more. But once the reader opens the book,
he understands too how they did it--about 650
whopping words per page! The cover for this
remarkably thin volume features the usual
deerstalker, magnifying glass, and pipe in the
foreground and dead trees and howling dog in the
background, all surrounded by a fog.

Lancer Books decided in 1967 to release
their own edition in their Magnum "Easy Eye"
series (13-407, 95¢). The impressionistic
cover painted in muted blue, purple, and green
colors by an artist whose name looks like
Storey(?). The cover features a stern-faced
Sherlock Holmes in the foreground and a red-eyed
hound, silhouetted by the moon in the background.
I believe this was the only Lancer printing.

Dale Books also published their own edition.
The cover for their 1978 edition features a pro-
file of Holmes with deerstalker and pipe and like
the Lancer cover, is stylized. This $1.25
edition was billed as "A Dale Classic."

Ballantine Books also chased the Hound.
Their 1975 edition was released as a "Ballantine
Mystery Classic" and sold for $1.25. The
caricature cover by Anderson has Holmes and
Watson in appropriate attire standing side by
side but facing opposite directions. This
Ballantine edition went through at least two
printings, perhaps more.

41

Anderson

THE HOUND OF THE BASKERVILLES

INTRODUCTION BY DON PENDLETON

Ballantine 24718

copyright page

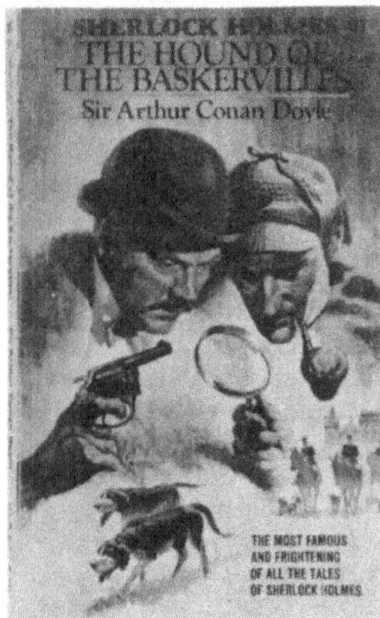

Gabriele

SHERLOCK HOLMES
THE HOUND OF
THE BASKERVILLES
Sir Arthur Conan Doyle

THE MOST FAMOUS
AND FRIGHTENING
OF ALL THE TALES
OF SHERLOCK HOLMES

A Belmont Tower Book

copyright page

Sometime after the Ballantine edition,
Belmont Tower released their own edition of
THE HOUND OF THE BASKERVILLES (50951, $1.25).
This interesting cover by "Gabriel" features
an unmistakable Basil Rathbone Holmes and
a Nigel Bruce Watson. Watson is holding a gun
and Holmes a magnifying glass. The most striking
thing about the Belmont Tower edition is that
the exact same plates from the Ballantine edition
were obviously used. One wonders if Belmont
Tower had Ballantine's permission, most probably
not. The plagiarism is quite obvious when one
examines the introduction.

Introductions and prefaces are common with
such classics as THE HOUND OF THE BASKERVILLES.
But of all the editions cited here, only three
have an introduction: The Scholastic Library
edition has an introduction by Herbert Brean who
is a mystery writer and former executive vice
president of the Mystery Writers of America.
The Airmont edition has an introduction by
Isidore Goldstein who is credited as being "Chair-
man, Dept of English Benjamin Franklin High
School." -- You would have thought Airmont could
have done better. The only other edition with
an introduction is Ballantine's. Their
introduction is by Don Pendleton who is well
known for his Executioner series. Ballantine is
the only edition which copyrighted their introduction which reads, "Introduction copyrighted
1975 by Don Pendleton." This copyrighted introduction leads us back to the Belmont Tower
plagiarism. On the copyright page and the title
page of the Belmont Tower edition, the copyright
statement of Pendleton's introduction is noted.
However, Belmont Tower didn't print the actual
introduction because that would have violated
copyright. The copyright for the story itself
has long run out and belongs to the public
domain which is why the nine paperback publishers
mentioned above all had a hand in writing the
paperback publishing history of THE HOUND OF THE
BASKERVILLES.

The Paperback Originals
Of Philip K. Dick
by Don Z. Block

For the paperback collector who enjoys reading science fiction, Philip K. Dick offers the
best of both worlds. He may be the greatest
science fiction writer this country has produced, and twenty-seven of his forty-one published works are paperback originals. Moreover,
these paperback works, unlike the hardcovers,
are not impossible to obtain. (The hardest-to-
find Dicks are probably the hardcover firsts of
TIME OUT OF JOINT, A HANDFUL OF DARKNESS, A MAZE
OF DEATH, and DO ANDROIDS DREAM OF ELECTRIC
SHEEP.)

The effect of a Philip K. Dick book is
chillingly unique. Dick's hero is usually a
decent, ordinary guy, a "minor man"; the evil
person or thing is usually superpowered.
The reader thus identifies with a character whom
he cares for but who is extremely vulnerable.
When this character must deal with the evil one,
him together with the reader, experiences pure
terror. It is par for the course to read a
Dick work and to become numb with fear. It is
common for a Dickian hero to say, "I give up,"
but it is just as common for him to change his
mind and to resume the fight.

What the Dickian hero must confront is truly
horrible. It can be a world running backwards
in time, a world in which the new born emerge
from the grave and gradually shrink to nothing-
ness as they grow younger (COUNTER-CLOCK WORLD).
It can be a world shaped by the psychotic per-
ceptions of sick individuals (EYE IN THE SKY,
CLANS OF THE ALPHANE MOON). Or it can be a
world, not simply distorted, but actually trans-
formed by drugs (THE THREE STIGMATA OF PALMER
ELDRITCH, A SCANNER DARKLY, NOW WAIT FOR LAST

44

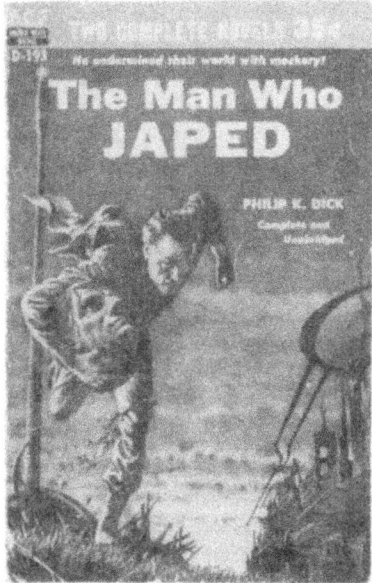

Ed Emsh

Ace Doubles by P. K. Dick

45

YEAR) and by lies (THE PENULTIMATE TRUTH, THE SIMULACRA, "If There Were No Benny Cemoli").

Dick's villains are fascinating because they appear to be harmless. This deceptiveness makes them even more terrifying when their full powers become apparent. In DR. BLOODMONEY, Bluthgeld seems to be no more than a lunatic who thinks he can destroy the world simply by willing it. Hoppy Harrington, armless and legless and having a cute alliterative name, seems to be a pathetically handicapped person, more likely to be harmed than vice versa. A child in THE COSMIC PUPPETS proves to be deadly. In SOLAR LOTTERY, the assassin who is selected to kill an idealistic politician seems to be physically unequipped to complete his mission. However, in one amazing scene, he suddenly takes off, literally takes off, and reveals dramatically his (or should I say its) full potential for evil. Dick makes you underestimate the power of evil, and because you are not ready for it, the full horror of it hits you with greater impact.

Dick relieves the horror with his optimism -- most of his endings are positive -- and with his sense of humor. In THE DIVINE INVASION, a soap opera character struggling with two bug-eyed spiders cries out: "Get your fucking mandibles off me!" (p. 39). In COUNTER-CLOCK WORLD, people sit down to breakfast before empty cereal bowls. When a vicious rug attacks its owner in "Colony," the victim says, "That's my rug. I brought it from Terra. My wife gave it to me. I--I trusted it completely" (in THE BEST OF PHILIP K. DICK, p. 135).

I have read every work Dick has had published and would highly recommend all but three (DR. FUTURITY, THE VARIABLE MAN, THE BOOK OF P.K. DICK). Thirty-seven out of forty is a high percentage of quality. Who else has written so much so well? It is no wonder that

46

THE SIMULACRA
PHILIP K. DICK

The Simulacra by P. K. Dick (Ace F301)

47

Dick's recent death devastated his many fans.
Tragically, Dick died right before the release
of the movie "Blade Runner" (the Hollywood
version of DO ANDROIDS DREAM OF ELECTRIC SHEEP?)
and right in the middle of a creative hot streak.
It is my guess, however, that Dick's works will
survive, just as his characters manage to do.
And, since the bulk of his work first appeared
in paperback, clearly the paperback industry --
Ace in particular -- deserves part of the credit
for making the world aware of the genius of
Philip K. Dick.

An Alphabetical Checklist
P.K. Dick's Paperback Originals

Novels
1. CLANS OF THE ALPHANE MOON (Ace F-309, 1964)
2. THE COSMIC PUPPETS (Ace D-249, 1957)
3. COUNTER-CLOCK WORLD (Berkley X1372, 1967)
4. THE CRACK IN SPACE (Ace F-377, 1965)
5. DR. BLOODMONEY (Ace F-337, 1965)
6. DR. FUTURITY (Ace D-421, 1960)
7. EYE IN THE SKY (Ace D-211, 1957)
8. GALACTIC POT-HEALER (Berkley X1705, 1969)
9. THE GAME-PLAYERS OF TITAN (Ace F-251, 1963)
10. THE GANYMEDE TAKEOVER (Ace G-637, 1967)
        with Ray Nelson
11. THE MAN WHO JAPED (Ace D-193, 1956)
12. MARTIAN TIME-SLIP (Ballantine U2191, 1964)
13. OUR FRIENDS FROM FROLIX 8 (Ace 64400, 1970)
14. THE PENULTIMATE TRUTH (Belmont, 92-603, 1964)
15. THE SIMULACRA (Ace F-301, 1964)
16. SOLAR LOTTERY (Ace D-103, 1955)
17. THE UNTELEPORTED MAN (Ace G-602, 1966)
18. VALIS (Bantam 14156, 1981)
19. VULCAN'S HAMMER (Ace D-457, 1960)
20. WE CAN BUILD YOU (DAW 14, 1972)
21. THE WORLD JONES MADE (Ace D-150, 1956)
22. THE ZAP GUN (Pyramid R1569, 1965)

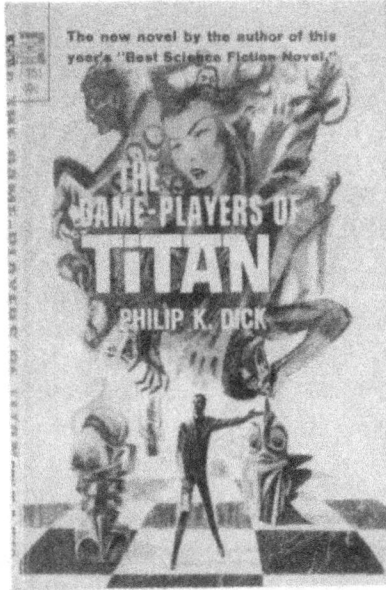

Jack Gaughan

Books in Ace F series by P. K. Dick

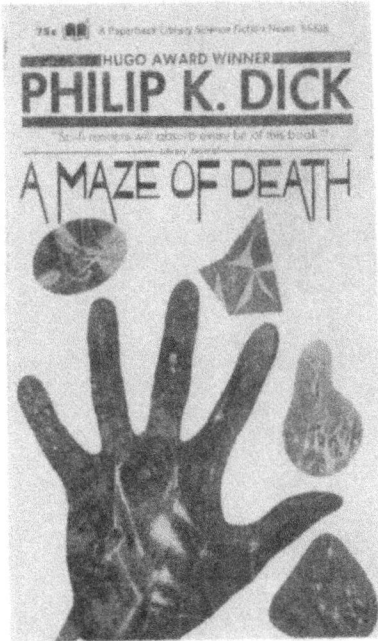

Jack Gaughan

A Paperback Library
book by P. K. Dick

A Pyramid SF book
by P. K. Dick

Short Story Collections

23. THE BEST OF PHILIP K. DICK (Ballantine 25359, 1977)
24. THE BOOK OF PHILIP K. DICK (DAW 44, 1973)
25. THE GOLDEN MAN (Berkley 04288, 1980)
26. THE PRESERVING MACHINE (Ace 67800, 1969)
27. THE VARIABLE MAN (Ace D-261, 1957)

My sources for the checklist are my own collection and the very thorough bibliography compiled by Daniel J.H. Levack, PKD: A PHILIP K. DICK BIBLIOGRAPHY (Underwood/Miller, 1981).

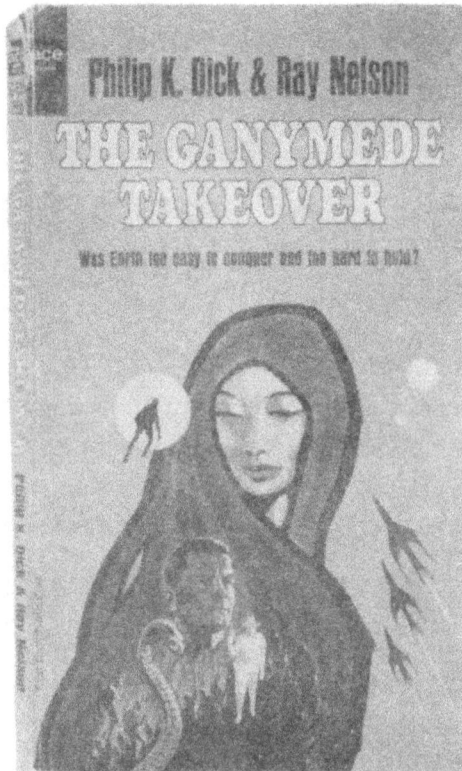

The Ganymede Takeover by P. K. Dick (Ace G-637)

More on P. K. Dick
by Shawn Loudermilk

P. K. Dick's first novel, SOLAR LOTTERY, is an Ace double and a paperback original. Since 1955, Ace has published 17 of Dick's books, all paperback originals. And of the 14 different American paperback publishers which have published Dick, Ace takes credit for over 60% of his paperback originals. The closest competitor is Berkley with only 3 paperback originals.

	Originals	Reprints
Ace	17	0
Berkley	3	1
Ballentine	2	2
Bantam	1	3
Belmont	1	1
DAW	2	1
Dell	0	7
Leisure	0	1
McFadden	0	2
Manor	0	2
Paperback Library	0	1
Popular Library	0	1
Pyramid	1	0
Signet	0	1

Ace's dominance is not surprising since in the 1950s Ace and Berkley were the clear leaders in SF paperback publishing. In his PKD bibliography (Underwood/Miller, 1981) Daniel Levack says "[the] SOLAR LOTTERY version differs considerably from [the] WORLD OF CHANCE version. Ace wanted revisions and Rich & Cowan wanted revisions, both different, so the author satisfied them both." Donald A. Wollheim, then

Hugo Award Winner

PHILIP K. DICK

DO ANDROIDS DREAM OF ELECTRIC SHEEP?

"Eminently exciting"—*The Newark News*

Alive yet not living, they sought to pass as humans
and seize man's dying earth

A Signet SF book by P. K. Dick

52

editor at Ace and the person who selected the
title SOLAR LOTTERY, says that Ace did not ask
for revisions. Wollheim stated in a recent
interview with PQ that PKD's works all fit
together very tightly and that "you couldn't
change any of it because it would tear the book
apart." Concerning SOLAR LOTTERY, Wollheim
added, "A lot of Philip K. Dick is in that book."

The list of paperback originals preceding
this article does not include the foreign
paperback original short-story collections.
The stories had appeared in English periodicals
but were first collected in book form in foreign
paperback translations. There were at least
six of these, including French, Italian, and
Dutch. These translations are indicative of
P. K. Dick's popularity overseas. Dick's
THE MAN IN THE HIGH CASTLE, first published
in hardback by Putman in 1962 and in paperback
by Popular Library in 1964 and Berkley in 1974
has been translated into at least 11 different
languages.

THE MAN IN THE HIGH CASTLE won Dick his
first major award, the 1963 Hugo for best
novel. His other awards include the 1975
John W. Campbell award for best novel for FLOW
MY TEARS, THE POLICEMAN SAID (a Doubleday
hardback, 1974; a DAW paperback, 1975, 1976,
1981) and the 1979 Graouilly d'Or Award for
best novel for A SCANNER DARKLY (a Doubleday
hardback, 1977; a Ballantine paperback, 1977).

In addition, Dick has been nominated for
a half dozen or so awards. DO ANDROIDS DREAM
OF ELECTRIC SHEEP? was nominated for the 1968
Nebula for best novel. It was originally published in hardback by Doubleday in 1968, then
in paperback by Signet in 1969 and 1971, and
by Ballantine in 1982 under the title BLADE
RUNNER. DO ANDROIDS DREAM OF ELECTRIC SHEEP?
was made into a movie and released in the
summer of 1982 also under the title BLADE RUNNER.

It is common in Hollywood for movie and book versions to have major differences. But with BLADE RUNNER the movie and BLADE RUNNER the book ("ANDROIDS..."), the differences are beyond major; they're different stories.

In the July 1982 issue of FANTASY NEWSLETTER, Alan Ryan says that Dick was made an offer to suppress republication of his book in favor of a tie-in novelization of the screenplay. Ryan says, "the offer was for more money than he'd ever gotten in his life. He turned it down." Ryan quotes Dick as saying, "You just can't do that. You can't kill the written word."

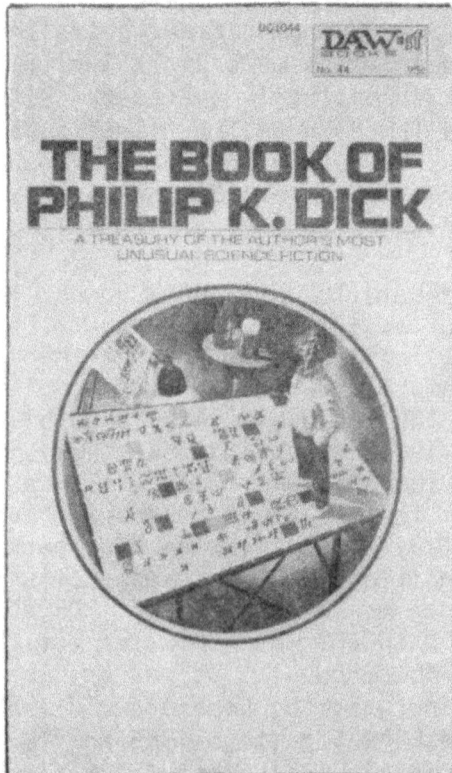

The Book of Philip K. Dick (Daw #44)

Letters

Dear Billy:

I enjoyed the articles in the latest PQ and have two pieces of information to pass on to your contributors. Piet Schreuders may like to take a look at the cover of Thriller Novel Classic #30, Charles A. Leonard's THE SECRET OF THE SPA, which utilizes the Alan Ladd photo but in mirror reverse. An illustration of this cover appears on page 369 of Hancer's PRICE GUIDE.

Daniel Roberts may be interested to know that his erratum #8, the wordless spine of Gold Medal #221, turns up on another Gold Medal book but probably with full intent. GM #323, John D. MacDonald's THE NEON JUNGLE, has a spine that bears no print other than the book number and a large T (presumably a distribution symbol). But the unique thing about this book is that it sports a full pictorial wrap-around cover illustration. So, did the layout personnel simply forget the spine lettering, or did they willfully omit it? One thing is for sure--the cover as it exists now is a real rarity among early paperbacks and a visual delight. Even the boxed-in back cover blurb is worth a smile:

> Said MICKEY SPILLANE: "I WISH I HAD WRITTEN THIS BOOK" Mickey was talking about John D. MacDonald's THE DAMNED
>
> Well . . . here is an even greater novel THE NEON JUNGLE by the same author

Well . . . those were the days. Take care till next time.

Sincerely,
Lawrence Abbott
4044 Chestnut St.
Philadelphia, PA 19104

Dear Billy:

I enjoyed the latest PQ; it had a nice balance, as most issues do. I enjoyed the interview with T. V. Olsen; though I wasn't familiar with his works, I became interested as a result of reading the interview. Don Hensley's checklist of the Avon Classic Crime Collection was also welcome. William O'Connell's examination of paperback editions of Gustave Flaubert's SALAMBO was excellent; I'd like to see more analyses of single titles. Where did O'Connell get the information about print runs? He mentions, for example, that the first Berkeley printing of SALAMBO was 151,000 copies. I've found that publishers are extremely reticent about releasing such data.

Dan Roberts' Errata was interesting. About #10-- Dell's edition of SPILL THE JACKPOT. I've never saw any edition with the "1" in "619" correct. And there was only one printing. Roberts notes that it would be useful to know how many editions of the printing were run off before the error was corrected. That information is unlikely ever to surface: no one at Western Printing & Lithographing, who printed the books (or other printers, I'm sure) was likely to stop the presses and count! I don't think we're ever going to get information like that for mass-market products.

Readers of PQ might be interested to know that Greenwood Press has accepted two books by me about the early Dell Paperbacks. The first book is entitled PUTTING DELL ON THE MAP: A HISTORY OF THE DELL PAPERBACKS, 1942-1962. It should be about 125-150 pages, with illustrations (b/w only, no color, I'm sorry to say). It's essentially a chronological appraisal of the books, with detailed chapters on the early front covers and the back-cover maps. One chapter discusses the books produced from 1962-1982, although that period is not my central concern.

The other book is a sort of companion volume:
DELL PAPERBACKS, 1942 TO MID-1962: A CATALOG-
INDEX. It has 450 camera-ready pages that I
typed, listing the books by series, indexing
the contents by author, titles (anonymous), cover
artist, subject, map, etc. No full title index
is included; there wasn't room. An introduction
is included as well: about 25-30 pages. Four
pages of illustrations should also appear.
Originally I had one enormous manuscript, which
took me six years to complete. My editor at
Greenwood suggested I split it. The history of
Dell will be included in Dell's "Contributions
to the Study of Popular Culture." The catalog-
index will be "A Greenwood Press Reference Book."
the two are meant to be used together, of course,
but they can be used independently of one another
as well. I hope paperback collectors find the
books of value. If I had a publisher willing to
invest a lot of money, I'd have done things
differently: color illustrations, for example,
even an illustration of each cover and map. But
I'm satisfied with things as they are. The books
should be out in early 1983. I have no idea
about prices, but I think the catalog-index will
be expensive. I'm trying to convince Greenwood
to publish the history as a paperback, with as
low a price as possible.

Sincerely,
Bill Lyles
77 High St.
Greenfield, MA   01301

60's Sleeze
(Adult Paperbacks 1960-68)

PRICE $2.00 (refundable with order)

TOM NIGRA   865 DIANE COURT   WOODERIDGE, N.J.   07095   PHONE: (201) 634-7105

This 32 page catalogue is the most comprehensive listing of the Esoteric-Erotica which flourshed in the 1960's that I know of. Hopefully, it will serve a dual purpose as a catalogue/check list for the over 2500 books listed from over 100 different publishers. Listed are most of the major publishing house titles (ie. Beacon, Midwood, Nightstand) and what seems to be complete runs of some of the lesser known publishers (ie. Clover Reader, Kozy Books, etc.(. Some of these series' started in the 50's (Newsstand, Bed Time, etc.) but most of them began and ended in the 1960's. Here is some truly "virgin" territory for the more adventurous book hunter.

The following publishers are listed:

After Hours	Fluer de Lis	Nitey-Nite Books	Sundown Reader
All Star	France Books	Novel Books	Swan Pub.
Athena Beacon	French Line (FEC)	Nite Time Criginals	Tempo Pub.
Bachelor Books	Galaxy Books	Night Shadow	Topaz Series
Bedside/Bedtime Books	Golden Books	Pad Library	TR Press
Bee-Line Books	Good Book	Pagan Criginals	Triumph
Boudoir Books/Classics	Greenleaf Classics	Paraiso Books	Tropic
Brandon House	Headline Books	Parliament	Tropic/Saber
Carousel Books	Hi-Hat Books	Period Publications	Tuxedo
Chevron Books	Holloway House	Phantom Books	Twilight Reader
Chariot	Idle Hours(Corinth)	Pike Books	Unique Books
Canyon	Impact Books	Pillar Books	Uptown Books
Clover Reader	Intimate Editions	Pillow Books	Valentine
Companion Books	Jade Books	Playtime Books	Vanguard
Corsair	Lantern Books	Pleasure Reader	Venice Pub.
Crescent	Late-Hour Books	Publishers Export Co.	
Crime-Adventure Series	Lancer Books	Rapture Books	Viceroy Pub.
Diary Books	Liesure Books(Corinth)	Raven Books	Victorian
Domino	Magenta	Rendevous Reader	Classics
Dove	Magnet Books	Rex Books	Wee-Hours
Edka	Mask Reader	Room Mate Books	Wisdom House
Ember/Ember Library	Mercury Books	Royal Line	Wizard Books
Emerald Reader	Merit Books	Saber Books	Zebra Books
Epic	Midnight Reader	Satan Press	
Europa	Midwood	Scarlet Reader	
Evening Reader	Macfadden	Scorpion Books	
Exotic	National Library	Social Behavior Books	
Fabian	Neoteric Books	Socio Text Books	
First Niter	Newsstand Books	Specialty Books	
Fitz Publications	Nightstand Books	Spotlight Books	
Flame	Nite-Lite Books	Stardust Books	

ALL BOOKS ARE VF/NM & $3.00 each 4/$10.00 unless indicated

POSTAGE: $1.50 for 1st 3 books 10¢ per Additional (this includes insurance)

DISCOUNTS: 20.00 - 50.00 postpaid
            50.00 -100.00 postpaid plus 10%
            100.00 -150.00 postpaid plus 10%
            150.00 -200.00 postpaid plus 10%
            200.00 - wholesale prices available: inquire

ALTERNATES: are stongly recomended since items are one of a kind

ADULTS ONLY: Age statement required for most titles, so please do so.

HE INTERNATIONAL PAPERBACK
MAILING LIST

<u>contains:</u>

1000 NAMES
TOTAL PRICE
$50⁰⁰
post paid

- •PHONE NUMBERS (When Available)
- •MAIL-ORDERS DEALERS W/PRICE LISTS.
- •WANT LISTS & SEARCH SERVICES.
- •PUBLICATIONS
- •CATALOGS
- •SPECIAL INTERESTS LISTED, i.e., VINTAGE, MYSTERY
  SF & F, etc.

AND

•AN INTERNATIONAL LISTING OF COLLECTOR'S
AND DEALERS FROM THESE COUNTRIES:

AUSTRALIA	CANARY ISLANDS	NETHERLANDS
CANADA	BRITISH COLUMBIA	SCOTLAND
ENGLAND		SWEDEN
IRELAND		TURKEY
JAPAN		USSR

THE INTERNATIONAL PAPERBACK
MAILING LIST
P.O. Box 16758
Phoenix, Az. 85011

_____
NAME

_____
ADDRESS

I enclose $50. Please send your international
paperback mailing list immediately.

_____
TOWN   STATE   ZIP

www.ingramcontent.com/pod-product-compliance
Lightning Source LLC
Chambersburg PA
CBHW021224020426
42331CB00003B/458